CAERLEON

'Scenes Recalled'

A Look Through Ages of Change

by Norman Stevens

Foreword by
Rosemary Butler
Member of the National Assembly for Wales

Old Bakehouse Publications

Abertillery

First published in September 2001

ISBN 1 874538 14 X

Published in the U.K. by
Old Bakehouse Publications
Church Street,
Abertillery, Gwent NP13 lEA
Telephone: 01495 212600 Fax: 01495 216222
www.mediamaster.co.uk/oldbakebooks

Made and printed in the UK
by J.R. Davies (Printers) Ltd.

Foreword

by Rosemary Butler
Member of the National Assembly for Wales
Former Secretary for Education and Children
Caerleon Councillor 1973-1999 Mayor of Newport 1989-90

'I shall always esteem it as the greatest piece of fortune that has fallen to me' wrote Arthur Machen *'That I was born in that noble, fallen, Caerleon-on-Usk in the heart of Gwent... when my eyes were first opened in childhood they had before them the visions of an enchanted land'*.

Perhaps some of the enchantment of Victorian Caerleon has been lost over the last century and a half (and in truth life then must have been very hard) but something of the magic can be recaptured when elderly residents who were children in Caerleon describe their memories of sheep being herded through Mill Street, the racecourse on Welsh Grand National Day, the excavation of *'Arthur's Round Table'* and collecting the morning milk from Lodge Farm.

I was born in the mining valleys but I have made my home in Caerleon for well over 30 years and even I can remember when there were no schools on Lodge Hill, when the buses terminated in Gwladys Place (and tickets to Newport cost ten old pence) and when the Brades still stood on Ponthir Road.

I, like Arthur Machen, believe that Caerleon is very special. Remnants of its awesome history are all around us (the steep ramparts of the Bronze Age Fort are just yards from the bottom of my garden) but at the town's centre the new University pioneers research into the most advanced aspects of new technology. In Caerleon we have both a unique Roman amphitheatre and one of the world's finest golf courses. Our town is also home to a vibrant community that I have been proud to represent, firstly as a councillor at Newport Civic Centre between 1973-99 and now a Member for Newport West at the National Assembly for Wales. Having been closely involved in Caerleon's affairs for many years I was delighted when Norman Stevens, an old friend, asked me to write the foreword for this his most recent book on Caerleon. It is fascinating to look through the pages, I'm intrigued to see that some of the more recent photographs are of events which I attended (is that my foot?) or even organised. On the other hand the 19th Century Caerleon we see in the photographs is still unmistakably recognisable and we can compare the faces of the now sadly forgotten school children, shopkeepers and sportsmen and sports women with our present day neighbours and friends.

Norman has provided us with a wonderful record of some of the many men and women who have had the good fortune, so well described by Arthur Machen, of living in Caerleon. My reaction now is to sort through my own photographs in preparation for Norman's next book.

Introduction

Compiling my second book of Caerleon photographs has been a great pleasure, in that it has allowed me to meet so many more of its residents and friends. Many sharing my desire to preserve and present in photographic form, memories, incidents, activities and personalities whether individual or in groups at work, or at play. It is only through fortunate chance often, that some aspects of Caerleon life and change have been recorded, often by personal family photographs and hobby interests.

Even at this present time, today's life and changes in fashions, commercial shop enterprises, road lay out changes reflect the way we live, work and play which will be looked back on with mixed emotions as time passes by and especially by the generations to come, who will in turn create their own heritage of memories and comparisons.

It is heartening that more and more of the residents whose families have been here for generations are appreciating the importance of their family photographs and are helping to preserve their heritage by allowing them to be shared and recorded. It is hoped that with the on-going enthusiasm shown so far, that a third book will be undertaken, incorporating the photographs offered but not used in this book because of similarity of subject but still worthy of preservation and publication.

In anticipation of your willingness to assist in future recordings of our past and my grateful sincere thanks to those who have participated so far, I would re-emphasise that I do not need to take away any items etc., but can photograph them, by arrangement, in your own home so that they never leave your possession, realising how much sentimental value can mean.

Again many thanks

Norman Stevens

11 Home Farm Close, Caerleon, Gwent. NP18 3SH   Tel: 01633 420187

Dedicated to
Fred W. Carey 1896-1989
Headmaster 1942-1959, Brynglas Secondary School, Newport, Mon.

whose moral integrity and selfless dedication to the future generations
of young people in his care, left a lasting if sometimes unconscious
set of values to guide them in life.

He served with courage in the trenches of the First World War
with the 1st Monmouthshire Regiment
and experienced the horror and futility
and survived, determined that the world be a better place.

Caerleon

Contents

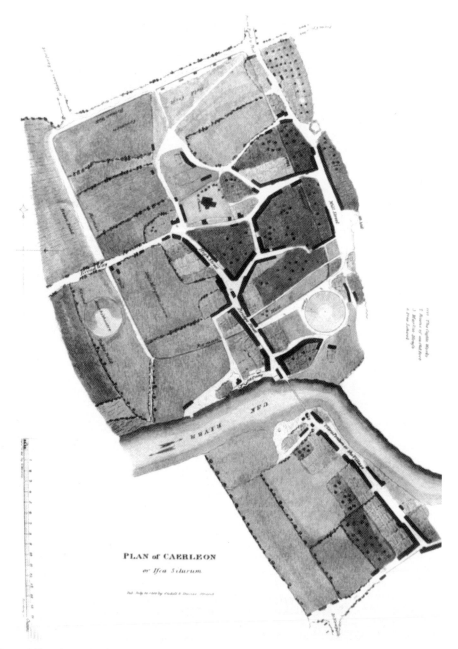

Plan of Caerleon, Published July 20th 1800 by Cadell & Davies, The Strand, London

Most of the descriptive names are haphazardly placed. The dense black areas shown following the road or street ways are places of habitation.
At the junction of Bridge Street, High Street and Cross Street, in the Square was the medieval market building, first recorded as being built in 1622 by Phillip Hughes of Caerleon who held the lease of much land also to collect tolls on fairs, markets and produce.
In 1653 it was described as a fine handsome building with freestone pillars standing in the Market Square outside The Bull Inn.
Around 1830 it was reported to have collapsed and market days ceased. The four freestone pillars were used in the crypt of the old museum as support to the floor built in 1850 with the rest of the old building materials being incorporated in the construction.

From The Bridge to The Square

'*Cleveland*' motor spirit being delivered by a Leyland tanker to the Hanbury Garage.
The photograph dates from around 1929 when R.R. Bennett was the proprietor.

'*Bennett's Garage*' 1950s, '*Service with a Smile*' (We're Going Well, We're Going Shell!)
1960s TV Ad jingle! Talking to customers is Gordon Bennett and replenishing the oil
is Marjorie Bennett. In the picture are some motor cars from the past such as a
Ford Zodiac in the background and an Austin A40 on the forecourt. Notice too a Vespa
scooter next to the 2-Stroke supply pump, also the traffic lights column for
controlling traffic crossing the bridge.

Hanbury Garage 1965 with more modern petrol pumps installed. Just behind the *'Mini'* about to cross the bridge, are traffic lights specially for users of the garage.

Hanbury Garage from the bridge, 1965. The pump outside the building on the left dispensed paraffin. On the bridge the pavement has been removed from the left side and the roadway marked for two way traffic. The traffic lights have been removed and only the redundant column on the left remains.

Corner of Bridge Street (later High Street) circa 1884 shortly before demolition and replacement with the Roman Catholic Church and Manse of Saints David, Julius and Aaron.

1950s looking down the river with the *'Hanbury Arms'*, the medieval stone tower at its side. A nostalgic scene when boating was popular.

An articulated unit belonging to Syd Jenkins, Haulage Company of Newport, Mon. It came to grief negotiating the bend into High Street with a load of steel coils en route from Llanwern Steelworks to the Midlands in 1960. Sergeant 299 Royce Gardener supervises the traffic and recovery. Mrs. Reynolds, wife of local GP Dr. Reynolds, had a lucky escape, she had just entered the church of St. David, Julius and Aaron by the doorway where a coil had come to rest, she exclaimed *'The Lord was with me today'*.

Castle Street junction with High Street, December 1979. A Midi Bus on hire from Bournemouth Corporation Transport Department, an experimental service between Home Farm Estate to Alway and Ringland. There was a flat fare of 10 pence adults, 7 pence child and O.A.P. without much success and with losses of almost £30 per day it stopped after 68 days, with 1,958 passengers being carried for a total of £190.

Lodge Road/Roman Way on 3rd October 1998 and *'Shamrock Coaches'* provide the Newport Caerleon Newport Service No.2 during the Newport Corporation Transport bus drivers strike. Shamrock kept the fares!

'*Ffwrrwm*' transformed from an old stable yard into an oasis of interest and tranquility by Dr. Russell Rees M.D. and his wife Gillian. The enterprise features antiques, art gallery, café, goldsmiths, bridalwear and craft shops and also sculpture and carvings with a strong Celtic and Arthurian theme.

Ffwrrwm murals, painted by Graham Cross, recreating a typical Roman scene of AD 96 as legionnaires of the 2nd Augustan Legion guard the exact entrance to the south gate depicted as true to life as possible. Unveiled by the Right Honourable Peter Hain M.P. Minister for Wales Education on 10th August 1998.

Artist Graham Cross and Dr. Russell Rees discuss Caerleon and Roman history with The Right Honourable Peter Hain M.P.

Local artist Mr. Graham Cross, B.A. Hons. (Fine Art) who resides at Ashwell, Ultra Pontem and has lived in Caerleon for the past seven years is seen here alongside one of his masterful creations. Graham was born in Newport and taught art at Lliswerry High School before his retirement. He has had paintings purchased by Newport Art Gallery and also exhibited in the United States, plus exhibiting in private collections and having a one man show at Llantarnam Art Gallery.

Recent Memories of Trials and Tribulations

In July 1996, major sewer and water pipe renewals resulted in extensive and prolonged (over 3 months) disruption to traffic and business in the town. The work was necessary because of increasing demands on what in many parts was the original pipework laid down over 100 years ago. All traffic was diverted via Mill Street and Castle Street with traffic lights (two way flow). Work was finally completed on Wednesday 4th September 1996.

Literally like a steeple chase course, High Street looking towards the river.

1996 and now Mill Street and Castle Street are chosen for pipe renewal, High Street having been reopened. Two way traffic flow provided a unique experience for the local inhabitants after so many years of one way driving. Here traffic waits near the Memorial Gardens for lights to change allowing travel down the narrow High Street.

Emerging from High Street near the junction of Castle Street.

Sunday 1st September 1996 outside the *'White Hart Inn'*. Traders and residents enjoy a *'Street Breakfast'* as guests of *'Welsh Water'*, in the middle of the Square to mark the completion of renewal of more than a kilometre of sewage and water mains that had required all traffic being diverted.

M. & M. Griffiths, Newsagent, Tobacconist, Groceries, Wines and Spirits taken in 1978.

High Street in 1940 with an evident lack of prosperity. The shop to the left was Mr. and Mrs. Davies *'Drapers'* though now shown as an *'Art Shop'*, but next one down is Reggie Bateman's Hairdresser. It is said he charged fourpence for a pudding basin cut, and depending on your social standing which of the two hairbrushes he used on you. The one with bristle or, one worn down to the wood!

The Square in the late 1950s. House and building to the left were demolished in the 1960s to create a car park and in the middle of the Square is the war memorial complete with lamp and drinking fountain.

Carcases of lamb hang outside Mrs. Richardson's Butcher's Shop, High Street at the corner of White Hart Lane. The gentleman in the foreground is believed to be the photographer adding to the crowd! The ornate gas lamp over the doorway of the White Hart would be a magnificent sight when lit. Circa 1905, the boards stacked behind the railings are security shutters for the shop. The name *'Mathews'* is to be seen on the glass of the transom window over the doorway. S. & C. Mathews were listed in Kelly's Directory of 1908 as Grocers - High Street.

May 1937 and John Skuse's Butcher's Shop is decorated to celebrate the Coronation of King George VI. Also advertised are Newport Races at Caerleon for Monday and Tuesday.

The Bull Inn and Vile Bros described as *'Manufacturers of High Class Aerated Waters'* (Pop) delivery cart, circa 1900. The large building to the left was the Malt House in early years, the building between it and the pub was demolished in 1963 to create a car park. The sign painted on the wall indicates *'Good Establishment for Touring Cyclists'*.

A close-up of the premises to the right in Cross Street which became a shop before being taken over by W.J. Bennett as a Cycle & Motor Works in 1905.

August 1911, Caerleon Post Office, Cross Street. Left to right: Florence Sarah Green, Edwin Arnold Green (Postmaster and Proprietor), William Williams, Billy Bowman, ?, ?, ?, ?, ?, Fanny and Aggie Taylor. *'Letters from all parts arrive (from Newport) at 4.15am, 8.15am and 2pm! and are despatched thereto at 11.50am, 2.00pm, 5.45pm and 9.00pm'*! The premises were also used for the manufacture and sale of boots and shoes under the title *'Leicester House'*, having been a family business of J. Greens & Sons in 1899, when Edwin was described as House Agent and Assistant Overseer. In 1908, Edwin having inherited the business, his brother Joseph was also so described but with the added responsibility of *'Collector to the Urban District Council'*. The population at this date was 1,367 and a rateable value of £8,543.

The Bull Inn being re-roofed with new Welsh slates in 1998. Notice the massive original beams and trusses supporting the roof as they have since the 15th century; a sight not to be seen again for many years.

Change of Owners and Use

Summer 1978, High Street. The Copper Kettle Restaurant and Tea Shoppe and flared trousers are the fashion. This will now be more familiar as *'Drapers'* Wine Bar.

1978, Cross Street *'Maid Marian'* mini supermarket, now occupied by *'The Bagan Tandoori Restaurant'*.

Cross Street and the shop next to the Bull Inn has another change in use, to Mr. L.E. Avery, Family Butcher from 1954 to 1972.

1978, Cross Street again a change of use, here used by William Hill, Turf Accountant.

The Exotic East returns to Caerleon. It's 2000 years since the Romans led their elephants to the games in the amphitheatre. *'Ashuk Miah'* riding the elephant and his business partner *'Salladur Rahman'* walking alongside create excitement as they tour the town supported by a theatre group, Roman soldiers and fair maidens, celebrating the opening of their *'Bagan'* Tandoori restaurant in Cross Street, 28th August 1989.

Wide Loads passing through Narrow Streets

Some of the typical heavy or wide loads that used to be routed through Caerleon before the stone bridge at Llantarnam was replaced with an ex army *'Bailey Bridge'* to relieve the Caerleon-Usk-Monmouth route of very heavy loads. Above, a Foden Tractor unit is seen hauling a pair of machinery castings in 1943. It is parked up on the common prior to its journey down High Street. The little boy is John Wynn, great grandson of Robert Wynn, the founder of the company with left to right, H.P. Wynn, Ted Morris (trailer fitter), Bill Haywood (tractor driver).

Another heavy load on solid tyred double-bogied trailer at rest near the Town Hall in the 1940s. The rear bogie was steered by a second driver walking at the back.

1949 and two more loads powered by four tractor units, with ex-army *'Diamond T'* ex-tank units at the front and *'Scammell'* behind, waiting for motor cycle police escort alongside *'The Croft'* house, Goldcroft Common.

The scene below shows an enormous cargo heading for Newport Docks in 1980, with trailer assistant manoeuvring the large cylinder load using the steerable rear bogie. It was not unknown to have one's house altered occasionally!

February 1980, Bridgend to Liverpool Docks. *'Wynns of Newport'* with a very large packing case going through the Square. Large, not too heavy loads still came through the town until the recent pavement improvements in August 1999.

Wynn's drivers were renowned for their driving skills, as also were their walking guides. This consignment is being hauled by a *'Scammell Amazon'* tractor unit with registration number AHB 807T.

R.A.O.B. Caerleon Branch of the Royal Antidiluvian Order of Buffaloes outside The Bull Inn, before an outing circa 1920. The solid-tyred bus was owned by Ruben Bennett and garaged opposite The Priory.

Caerleon R.A.O.B. Branch ready to depart on another outing circa 1930 carrying their regalia in the case.

Late 1950s at a time when you could park your bike (complete with pump) and it would still be there intact upon returning and Morris Dancers could dance in the street.

1977 and the dig begins to uncover the Roman baths, Bull Inn.

Back Hall Street and Bert Niklasson's grocery shop now a hairdressing salon. Bert took over the shop from Mrs. Winmill in 1954 and retired in 1986. Standing outside are left to right, Edith Niklasson and Sofia Evans.

Reg Henry's Hairdressing Salon in the 1970s in Cross Street. It has since been the 'New Leaf' bookshop, an art gallery and now 'Hickory Dickory Dock Young Childrens Clothes Shop'.

Val Burnel-Jones, Antique Shop *'Gaslight'* where she specialised in quality Victorian, Edwardian and 1920s and 1930s ladies apparel and accessories, from 1980 until 1996, when ill health forced her to close. The property was sold in 1999 and has since been converted to a private house.

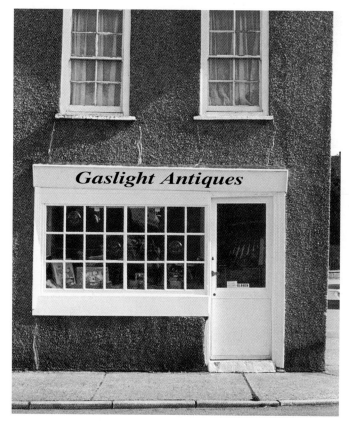

This picture of *'Gaslight'* was taken in 1980.

'*London Inn*' in Church Street as it appeared in the 1930s. Below is the same inn during the 1950s with customers heading for the door, at opening time. A very nice Humber Snipe Motor car is parked outside, a period when petrol was three shillings (15p) a gallon and a very extended lamp standard was there to cast an all round light on the Square. The inn is now a private house with playgroup premises adjoining to the right.

The Knorz family outside their home at 4 Castle Street, Caerleon in 1914. Left to right: Addie, Beatrice, Mrs. Emma Knorz and Arthur, family bakers in Caerleon for many years.

1921 the family has prospered and increased. Left to right: Mrs. Emma Knorz, Addie (Addeline), Mr. Charles Knorz, Bill (William). Front: Gladys, Beatrice and Arthur.

Mr. and Mrs. Knorz on their Golden Wedding Day.

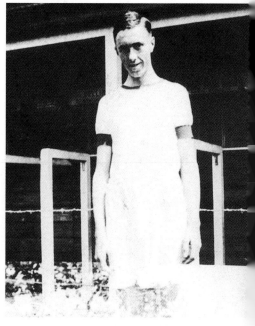

As a runner, Arthur in 1930 aged 16, outside the Tote on Caerleon Racecourse. He used to compete in 100 yards, 440 yards and mile races.

Arthur, aged 11 years holds the reins of the horse-drawn delivery cart outside their house and bakery in Backhall Street, now demolished but still the site of the present bakery. Cottages on the left in the background are now demolished and replaced with semi detached houses.

Master baker, Mr. Charles Knorz proudly shows his baking skills with his bread sheaf made for the harvest festival at St. Cadoc's Church. In business from 1920 until his death on December 23rd 1952, Arthur returned from the war and joined his father but ill-health forced him to close in February 1953.

Arthur Knorz 'The Baker' 1970 in retirement, proud of his garden and Caerleon Bowling Club Life Membership with his trophies.

Local Produce

Locally baked bread still available. The bakery in the 1970s and owned by William and Julie Ann Ford from 1988; the shelter and tables being removed by order of the council. A facility much missed and visitors to the shop will see the original iron oven doors set into the exterior wall as a feature of the past.

Taken in February 2000, the owners and staff all pictured inside the shop with the bakery at the rear. Left to right: Julie Ann Ford, William Ford, Heidi Ford, Kerry Freke and Carole Davies.

The Ampitheatre and Bear Pond

Horse-drawn grass cutter at work on the site of the amphitheatre in 1914. The subsequent excavation took place in 1927 by Dr., (later Sir) Mortimer Wheeler and his wife Mrs. Tesse Wheeler. In the driving seat is Tom Herbert, who owned several businesses in the area, including at various times, the 'White Hart' and 'Red Lion' inns. The little boy is Stanley, his son, aged five who was born in the 'Red Lion'. Between the rear of the horses and the grass cutter can be seen the above-ground remains of the stone walls of the amphitheatre. In the background on the right is 'The Priory'.

Between the Fosse Way and Barracks Field. Sunday 19th September 1999, Bear House (Field) Pond reappears after 50 years, what was for many generations a permanent feature for youngsters to play (in!). It disappeared years ago with the installation of drainage works in the surrounding area, but its re-appearance was caused by exceptionally prolonged rains and blockages in the drains. Enjoying a dip is Cocker Spaniel 'Phoebe' watched by Tracy Pritchard, her owner.

St. Cadoc's Church and Roman Museum circa 1905.

Caerleon Endowed School - Portraits Through The Years

Caerleon Endowed School, circa 1900.

Caerleon Endowed School, old boys first reunion, December 27th, 1923. A mixture of ages and some must have been pupils at the turn of the century. Who is the solitary lady at the back?

Caerleon Endowed School, Infants *'Second A'* (Second Year, Form A?) circa 1905. Pinafore dresses and boots were the fashion.

Caerleon Endowed Infants School known as the *'Town Band'*, 1950s.

Classroom in the Endowed School, 1923. A science cabinet is to be seen on the rear wall and at this time Mr. Evan Davies was Headmaster and Science Teacher.

Caerleon Endowed School, Infants Class 4 in the 1940s. Back row, left to right: Miss Talmadge, Billy Warren, ?, ?, May Morton, K. Jams, Joyce Pope, ?, ?, Angela Gulley, ? Jones, Ken Lewis, John Lentle. Third row: ?, ? Young, Shirley Lewis, ?, Bernard Burroughs, ?, ? Cox, ?, ?, ?, Teddy Waters, Arthur Powell. Second row: Christopher Carpenter, Beryl Carpenter, ? Vaughan, Barbara Gulley, ? Davies, Gwyneth Davies, Glyn James, ?, ?, ?, ?, ?. Front row: Glyn Watkins, Ruth Wollan, Tony Ansty, Sylvia Crossman, Shirley Richards, ?, ?.

Caerleon Boys Group II circa early 1940s.

Second Year IV circa early 1940s.

Class 2 Caerleon Endowed Infants 1943. Back row, left to right: Miss Talmadge, Kathleen ?, Joan Wollan, Barbara Anthony, Stephanie Edwards, ?, Brian Kilvington, ?, Val Burnell-Higgs. Middle row: ?, Zena Winmill, Jackie Winmill, Margaret Jones, Clifford Blythe, ?, ?, Sylvia Cressman, ?. Front row: ?, ?, ?, Leonard Wollan, Valerie Jones, Olive Kembrey, Blodwyn Williams, Pamela Duffield, ?.

Class 3 Infants 1943.

41

Caerleon Boys Group 3, circa early 1940s.

Caerleon Boys, circa late 1940s.

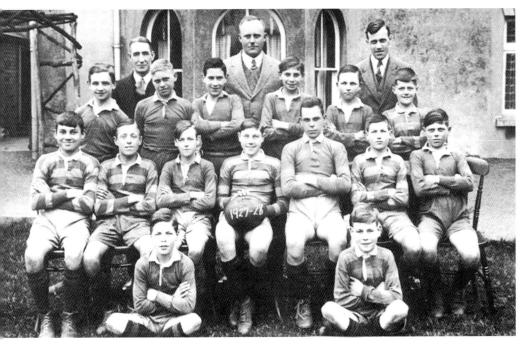

Caerleon Endowed School, Rugby Team 1927-28
Back row, left to right: Mr. Francis (Teacher), Mr. W.G. Lovatt (Headmaster), Mr. Deacon (Teacher). Middle row: Eric James, Cliff Pearce, ? Cook, Gomer Hopkins, ? Thomas, St. Cadoc's Home Boy. Front row: John Upton, ? Rossiter, Herbert Williams, Eric Baker, Cliff Tyrol, Albert Gear, Jim Davies. In Front: ? Jones and St. Cadoc's Home Boy.

Caerleon Endowed School, Rugby Team 1929-30
Back row, left to right: Mr. Cliff Francis (Teacher), Mr. Wilf Deacon (Teacher). Standing: Percy Jenkins, Ron Pearce, Tony Powell, Harold Pearce, John Parker, Jack Evans, Jack Carpenter and Gordon Wilkinson. Sitting: Les Carpenter, Arthur Young, Albert Gear (Schoolboy International), Mr. W.G. Lovatt (Headmaster), ? Jenkins, John Mapp and Glyn Bergam. Front: ? Pearce, Albert Young and Jimmy Dixon.

Caerleon Endowed School, Hockey Team 1926
Back row, left to right: Irene Richards, Molly ?, Louise Davies, Winnie Phillips, Mary Williams, Gladys Knorze. Third row: Margaret Evans, Win Horman, Elsie Nicholas, Amy Hall, Evelyn Morgan, Ethel Tarr. Second row: Tricia McDivat, Nellie Mayo, Dorothy Jones, Lily Lewis, Megan Blunt, Miss Tooze (Teacher), Beryl Arnold, Kitty Harris, Winnie Owen, Evelyn Neal. Front row: Edna Upton, Myra James, Ester Phillips, Lucy Gidman.

Caerleon Endowed Infants School kitchen staff, 1952. Left to right: Mrs. Dando, Mrs. White, Mrs. Pidgeon, Mrs. Miggins and Mrs. Williams.

Retirement presentation to Mr. David Havard and Mrs. Havard, Caerleon Endowed Infants Headmaster 1986.

National Figures and Local Politics

Monmouthshire Teachers Conference at the Endowed School 1950s. Rt. Hon. Aneurin Bevan P.C., M.P. seated centre, to his left Primrose Hockey M.B.E. (Head Teacher), Godfrey Rowlands, Chairman Caerleon U.D.C., Russell Green with Clerk to the Council, standing behind.

Labour Party stalwarts get together at the Town Hall with London HQ Representative to plan the 1964 Election campaign. Left to right: Jim Waggett, Don Stewart, Cwmbran visitor, Cwmbran visitor, Barbara Castle M.P., unknown, unknown, Jack Williams M.B.E.

Goldcroft Common 3rd May 1984 and a milk crate not soap-box oration. Dr. Russell Rees M.D. seeks to persuade that he is the man for the job as representative for Caerleon on Newport Council. He lost to the Conservative candidate by 243 votes, it was alleged at the time that a bogus Welsh Nationalist Candidate was put up by renegade young Liberals which affected the vote. The polling officer refused a rerun on the grounds of cost. Left to right: Ron Thompson, Catherine Philpot, Jeff Rees (Proprietor of 'New Leaf' bookshop, Cross Street), Dorothy Kirkwood, Mr. Powell, Russell Rees M.D., Helen Lofts, Sue Smith.

Priory Hotel 1974 and a final get-together of Past and Present Councillors of Caerleon Urban District Council. Back row, left to right: Terry Baldwin, Jim Waggett, Eric Kilvington. Third row: Brian Papps, Geoff Rowlands, John Duthie. Second row: Mr. Morris, Lillian Lewis, Jim Kirkwood, T. Tranter, Mr. Lloyd, John Pritchard, Val Burnell-Jones, J. Parker, Max Morrish (Clerk to U.D.C.). Front row: Colonel Horace Lyne, Chairman Steve Veal and Tom Shierson.

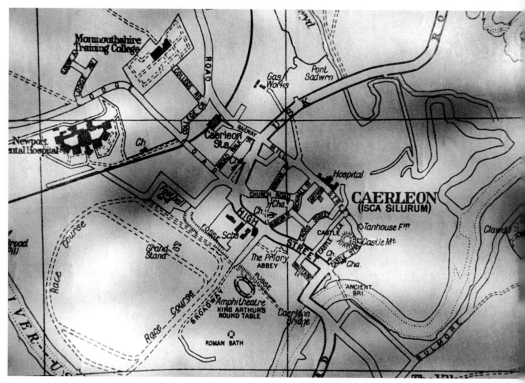

Ordnance Survey Map of the 1930s clearly showing the racecourse, this area is now part of the Comprehensive School and municipal golf course.

Caerleon Racecourse in the 1930s viewed from Caerleon Road, near Beaufort Road, Newport.

THE GRAND STAND AT CAERLEON RACES.

May 25th, 1931 *'A Great Day Out'*.

1932 the day's racing is over and the crowds leave the course via the main gate into Cold Bath Road. The photograph was taken from the first floor side window of *'Danebury House'* adjacent to Lodge Road. Charles Richards senior is in the foreground sporting an open necked shirt. The huts on the left were *'the mushroom farm'* a business started around 1946 by the brothers Russ and Don Green. It was closed down because of an infection after a few years. The premises were bought by Mr. Greenway, and the largest shed was converted into a bungalow for his own use, it has recently been extensively rebuilt and modernised.

Gordon Murray in 1941 and an empty grandstand and empty pocket!

Caerleon College, now University taken in the early 1950s. Standing in splendid isolation, the ever-expanding campus has seen much of the fields built on with accommodation and service blocks. To the middle right *'The Brades'* with the manager's house dating from the 18th century (2 chimneys) demolished 1979. In the background is the Star Brickworks with its now solitary chimney.

1952 Caradog Road later renamed Roman Way. The bush in the garden on the right was part of the field, the new houses were built around it!

1971, Lodge Road bridge over the railway with pedestrians on the narrow footpath. A Leyland Atalean Reg. PDW 98H, makes its way on the Caerleon Route 2 to Lodge Estate; these buses were Newport's first type to have front passenger loading and one-man operation being bought in 1970 and withdrawn and sold in 1981. On the left, notice the damage to bridge side near warning marker posts, a fairly common occurrence despite the white painted kerbs marking the hazard.

It's 1977 and the Lodge Road footbridge is being installed for the safety of pedestrians on a very busy road.

Caerleon Retired Persons Welfare Club

The club was opened on the 17th May, 1949 by Miss Radcliffe, who resided at the *'Priory'* Caerleon. Meetings were held in a wooden hut on Lodge Road (one of a number built during the war to house firemen of the National Fire Service, who manned the Fire Station in Mill Street), it being demolished at the end of hostilities. The hut was located where *'Isca Court'* is now built and there were 36 members at the opening, the subscription being threepence. A draw was held with 2 lbs of sugar as the prize. The club moved to the Town Hall in late 1972, meeting every Thursday evening when bingo, concerts and other events are put on. Membership has grown to between 80 and 100 and subscription is now £2.50 annually. Tea and biscuits are provided free and visitors are always welcome. At least four day-outings are enjoyed per year, together with free *'Christmas Dinner and Draw'* with every member receiving a gift. The 50th Anniversary of the club was celebrated at the Town Hall on 13th May 1999 where members were provided with a meal and entertainment. A welcome is extended to any retired persons over 50 years of age to join. For the last 10 years, Royce Gardener, a retired police sergeant (of Caerleon) has been Chairman.

Caerleon Retired Persons Holiday to Pontins Holiday Camp on the Isle of Wight 1973 Back row, left to right: Mrs. Edith, unknown, unknown, Mr. Eric Kilvington, Mr. George Wollan, Mr. Bert Anstey, Mr. Geoff Rowlands. Fourth row: Mr. Eric Newman, Mr. John Hopkins, Mr. Albert Harris, Mrs. Lillian Fox, Mrs. Cissie Hopkins, Mrs. Nancy Wollan, Mrs. Beatie Perkin, Mrs. Madge Coopey. Third row: Mrs. Doll Young, Mrs. Harris, Mrs. Flo Pritchard, Mr. Robson, Mrs. Edna Ford, Mrs. Gertie Batt, Mrs. Ernie Wollan, Mr. Coopey. Second row: Mr. Keene, Mr. Billankin, Mrs. Wright, Mr. Wright, Stan Glover, John (the driver), Rose Hall, Clarice O'Shea, Mrs. Cook, Mr. Cook. Front row: Mrs. Eric Newman, Mrs. Tom Keene, Mrs. Flo Davies, Mrs. O. Jones, Mrs. H. Kilvington, Mrs. Rene Anstey, Mrs. Win Crowden, Mrs. Marchant, Mrs. Alice Cook, Mrs. Daisy Tripp.

A V.J. celebration party which was held for retired persons in the Town Hall.

Caerleon Retired Persons Welfare Club during their 50 years Celebration Dinner held at Caerleon Town Hall on 13th May, 1999. On the top table facing the camera are Royce Gardener (Chairman), Herbert Niklasson, Doreen Vickery (Treasurer), Madelaine Daniels (Secretary), Raymond Llewellyn, Alan Whiting (Town Hall caretaker).

Caerleon Retired Persons Welfare Club
50 years Celebration Dinner held at Caerleon Town Hall on 13th May, 1999.

September 22nd, 1880 and local athletes pose outside the Town Hall. The barn in the background is in the grounds of what is now the Endowed School Infants Playground.

Carnival Time

Carnival Queen 1952. Back row, left to right: Ray Gibbens, Don Stewart, Ron Vaughan, Reg Johnson, George Phillips, George Pincher, Gilbert Ayliff, Mr. Lovatt, Bill Powell, Sergeant Bleese, Bill Cook, Gordon Murray, Ted Marchant. Front row: Miss Glass, Maureen Carver, Pam Cook, Marion Bergam, Beryl Teague, Maureen Jones, unknown. Girl on lorry Sonia Phillips.

Carnival 1977 with Catherine Teague as Andy Pandy.

Crowning the Carnival Queen in 1954. Left to right: Eric Kilvington with Beryl Teague being crowned by Chairman of the U.D.C., William Povall. Court Lady is Betty Hammet.

Ahoy me hearties! A pirate ship with a fearsome motley crew and Mr. Ted Marchant appearing in the 1956 Carnival.

Television Toppers Float 1955. Back row, left to right: Kathleen Strong, Gwyneth Keene, Iris Reader, Ann Brown, Mary Harry, Pat Rice. Front row: Marion Raines, Dorothy Williams, Joyce Williams, Maureen Singleton, Billie Watkins, Audrey Waters and Ern Hough as the cameraman.

Tiny Tots take tea in Victorian style 1955.

1957 with the '6-5 Special' Float. Back row, left to right: Brian Dixon, Carole Taylor, Kay Pritchard, Ann Teague, Graham Jamie, John Bowden, Andy Jones. Front row: Monica Williams, Eileen Chantler, Lillian Williams.

The Lodge Jazz Band 1956 on the common for the judging. Standing, left to right: unknown, Kay Pritchard, Carole Taylor, Geraldine Collins, Ann Teague, Lillian Williams, Yvonne Richards, Sonia Phillips, Veronica Keene, unknown, Francis Rollins, Monica Williams, Janice Vickery. In front: ? James, Vivian Asquith, John Wollan, David Hopkins, unknown, Alan Ahearne.

1959 Jack Harris's Commer Lorry at Roman Way ready for the parade of floats. Left to right: Chris Phillips, ? Bamford, Billy Teague, ? Dixon, ?, Edward Harry.

1963 judging taking place on Goldcroft Common. Left to right: Lyn Richards, John Wollan, Tony Wollan, Adrian Jones, Raymond Wollan, Godfrey Jamie, David Hopkins.

Saint Trinians Float at Lodge Avenue before the start of the carnival 1958. Left to right: Elizabeth Richards, Vera Teague, Florence Williams.

1953 Carnival. Audrey Waters as a *'Stick of Rock'*.

1946 Carnival. Walkers crossing Lodge Road Bridge. Left to right: John Freeburg (lovely lady), Charles Waters (parody of a Roman Centurion) and John Waggett (as a British toff).

1952 Carnival, picture taken at the football field. Left to right, standing: Recently demobbed soldier, One of Robin Hood's maidens, French girl, Nelson's cabin boy, Dutch girl, Swiss Miss, ?, Mountie and a rural maiden from the pig farm. Seated: An old schoolboy international footballer, straw-boater schoolgirl and a baby with a dummy.

Caerleon Comprehensive School *'Dinner Ladies'* 1989/90. Back row, left to right: June Adams, Tegwyn Vaughan, Jeanette Williams, Maureen Gibb, Lorna McDermot, Myrtle Tudor, Anne Arnold and Avelon Sutton. Middle row: Maureen Sherrin, Maureen Griffiths, Sandra Coldrick, Kathy Eynon, Ros Wookey, Sally Tebby, Joan Anderson, Janet Ripley. Front row: Pat Dixon, Anne Moloney, Gwyneth Westron, Susan Honeywell, Pat Smith, Cheryl Cashman, Jackie Dunk.

Lodge Road Area 1955, Children's Party held in grounds of Caerleon College. Among the children to be seen are Yvonne Richards, Janice Vickery, Geraldine Collins, Jennifer James, Andrew Jones, Jacqueline Parry, Johnny Bowden, Richard Jones, Edward (Dickie) Waters, Lyndon Pugh, Stephen Lloyd, Brian Dixon, Colin Jones, Michael Collins, Billy Strong, Kay Pritchard, Elaine Chandler, Marilyn Chandler, Gillian Bowden, Vivian Asquith, David Higgs, Nancy Wollan, Adrian Jones, Lyn Richards, Brenda Dickson, Margaret Reader, Jeffrey Reader and Martin Richards. 'Corona' pop supplied the paper hats.

Caerleon Comprehensive School - Distinguished Visitor

Visit to Caerleon Comprehensive School in 1987 by the Rt. Hon. Peter Walker, M.P., Secretary of State for Wales who is being addressed by Mr. Brian Medhurst, Head of the Upper School.

Headmaster Mr. Clarry Lapham introduces the Welsh Secretary to pupils of the sixth form, together with Mrs. Veronica Baynam now head of year seven. Mr. Lapham who joined Caerleon Comprehensive in 1987 sadly passed away in February 1995.

1955 The children's party at Caerleon College, held for those living in the nearby area. Back row, left to right: Beryl Carpenter, Kathleen Collins, Tegwyn Pugh and Maureen Collins. Third row: Jacqueline Parry, Margaret Dakin, Elaine Chantler, Kay Pritchard, Valerie Jones, Audrey Waters, Kathleen Strong, Marion Raynes, Maureen Singleton, Iris Reader. Second row: Gordon Richards, Robert Evans, Francis Hill, Jimmy Povall, John Harris. Front row: Martin Richards, David Higgs, Gillian Bowden, Adrian Jones, Lyn Richards, Jenny James, Nancy Wollan and Jeffrey Reader.

April 1981 Caerleon Comprehensive change to buttery style catering for the pupils. Kitchen staff demonstrate at a Parents evening the meals that will be available. The evening was sponsored by the 'Milk Marketing Board'.

Pancake Day, Activities on the Goldcroft Common

Goldcroft Common, Shrove Tuesday Annual Pancake Race 1979. Left to right: Joel Studley, ?, ?, ?, Katie Baggs, ?, Pat Maloney (nee Teague) with her daughter Keri, Ann Moloney with son Terance, ?, ?, ?, ?, ?.

Katie Baggs and Terance Maloney race to the finishing line with an enthusiastic Caroline Studley all smiles and a victors salute.

St. Cadoc's Hospital

An excellent overall view of St. Cadoc's Hospital during the early 1950s clearly showing the layout of the wards and administration buildings, grounds and Home Farm with well-tended fields. There is gradual in-filling along Lodge Road and Lodge Hill with its prefabs and there is just one motor car in the whole picture parked outside the main administration block.

To bring comfort and entertainment to residents, a *'BROWN'* six valve radio receiver and six loud speakers supplied to St. Cadoc's Hospital, 1920 by *'Harry Gillard'*, *'Wireless House'*, Cardiff Road, Newport.

A Christmas Greetings Card from one of the unfortunate patients to their loved relatives.

Royal British Legion - Caerleon Branch

11th November 1998 Royal British Legion, Caerleon Branch gather in the Memorial garden to honour the fallen. Back row, left to right: Doug Glass, Jim Povall, a serving visiting soldier, Arthur Knorz, W.R. Berts (standard bearer), Edward Cooper, Allan Fox, Lionel Watkins. Front row: Jim Waggett, Queenie Waggett, Councillor Jim Kirkwood, Jack Hard, Ron Morgan, Gordon Murray, Ken Rees, Donald Stewart, Ron Pearce, Henry West (Branch Poppy Fund Organiser).

Caerleon Branch of the Royal British Legion 1951 Parade at the Amphitheatre celebrating the Festival of Britain. Left to right: Mrs. V. Gough, Mrs. E. Jordan, Fred Griffin, Fred Shierson, James Weeks M.B.E., D.S.M., E. Davies, Tom Edwards, ? Davies, P. Griffin, G. Pike, D. Stewart, A. Povell, A.C. Ackers, Harry Wall, Les Hewinson and Mr. Edwards.

The Royal British Legion, Sunday 11th November 1994. The Caerleon Branch, formed on 23rd June 1924, passes through the Lychgate into St. Cadoc's Church after parading through Caerleon with other branches during a service to mark 75 years of the founding. *'They shall not grow old, as we who are left to grow old, age shall not weary them, nor the years condemn. At the going down of the sun and in the morning we will remember them.'*
'When you go home, tell them, for your tomorrows, we gave our todays.'

Goldcroft Common - Station Road and Railway Station

August 1996. The late John Skuse, Master Butcher and proprietor with the late John Griffiths, his skilled assistant, both courteous gentlemen who are sadly missed. With them is Donald Stewart and this was the last photograph taken before closure of the shop through ill-health which came on the 4th February 1998. The end of an era, a family business that served with pride for 77 years.

7th September 1998 the premises leased by Charles Spencer Stedman and extensively refurbished as 'Caerleon Barbers Shop' catering for male clients, with Debbie Pennell as the newly appointed manageress.

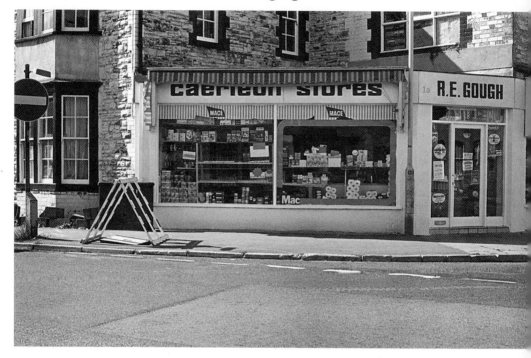

Station Road and the corner of Usk Road during the late 1960s or early 1970s. Below, what was a ladies hairdressing salon, with a Rover 2000 car neatly parked, the building has since been converted to a private residence.

Station Road, corner of Broadwalk in 1960. To be seen is Grocer and Baker A. Jones, a family business which closed in 1974. In the picture are some nice period cars and van, a Morris Minor, Ford Anglia van and a Morris Cowley saloon.

Railway Street (now Station Road) and Broadwalk in 1912. Left to right: Nessie Jones (Daughter), Mrs. Annie Jones (Mother and Proprietor), Garfield Jones (son), Herbert Jones (son), Frank Weston, Dorothy Jones (daughter).

Caerleon Railway Station

A selection of passenger railway tickets 2nd and 3rd Class, Single and return issued for journeys to and from Caerleon by the Great Western Railway and latterly British Railways (Western Region) with fares ranging from (pre decimal) 4 pence, 6 pence, 7 pence, 7½ pence and 8 pence, for adults and children. Below *'Same Day'*, *'Three Days and Monthly'* tickets.

Forecourt of Caerleon Station in the 1960s. The door on the left is the *'Lamp Room'*, used for storing and servicing the paraffin oil signal lamps. The larger door to the right is the main entrance to the Ticket Booking office. The Daily Mail *'Ideal Home Exhibition'* advert top left and British Railway's own advert urges potential travellers to *'Try our quick diesel services'*.

Summer of 1959, Caerleon Station, an express drawn by British Rail Engine, Britannia Class passes through on the down platform line. Note the signal post above the bridge parapet. This needed to be positioned the other side of the bridge and was exceptionally tall, in order that engine drivers could sight it on the long curve from Ponthir.

A diesel multiple unit stands at the up platform, with the signal indicating permission to proceed.

A warm July evening in 1956 and the down Birmingham Express, headed by a Hawksworth GWR Castle Class Locomotive passes the goods shed and signalman, Bryn Collier holding his box Brownie camera at the foot of the signal box steps. Bryn (inset, aged 17) started work on the GWR at 14 years of age as an engine cleaner in 1942, at 7 shillings (35p) per 56 hour week! He graduated to locomotive fireman at 16 years, then 12 years later changed to the signals' department serving a further 14 years, ending his service at Caerleon Signal Box. When he retired from the railway he worked for the Usk River Authority as Coxswain Water Bailiff from 1964-78.

British Railways Western Region, diesel multiple unit approaches Caerleon from Ponthir, in the 1960s.

1960, ex GWR Pannier Tank 3685 steams into the up platform at Caerleon, with a train of 20-ton, loose coupled mineral wagons. On the smoke box door written in chalk is *'Silver Queen'*. The single lamp on the side bracket of the buffer beam indicates that the train is a Class 9, used to pick up branch line freight.

A *'Grange'* class loco on a Birmingham Express passes Caerleon signal box 1960.

Passing through St. Cadoc's cutting before entering Caerleon Station. 45699 *'Galatea'*, an LMS engine of Jubilee Class on Great Western territory, 1960 Cardiff to Shrewsbury, which was routed via Panteg then on to Pontypool mainline. This engine is still in existence awaiting restoration.

April 1953, Caerleon Station and main lines with goods sidings to the right. Lower right can be seen, the chimney and safety valve cover of the daily pick up goods engine, Pontypool Road to Newport Alexandra Docks, shunting to collect empty wagons. Station Road and overbridge are seen in the background.

Coming up the long drag from the Usk River Crossing Bridge out of Newport, heading north past St. Cadoc's Hospital grounds, is a former London Midland and Scottish Stanier 8F railway engine pulling a mixed van and wagon train.

Express trains to the North passing on the up line through Caerleon Station, drawn by ex Great Western Railway, Castle Class locomotives, bearing two lamps on the buffer beam, and smoke box door signs M87 and M91, for the benefit of Signalmen routing them correctly as they pass their signal boxes. Circa early 1960s. The lettering in whitened stones on the grass banking are the initials B.R. (British Railways). This follows tradition when GWR and Coronation displays were initiated by station staff. Both pictures are of the 0800 hrs. Plymouth-Liverpool express.

April 30th 1962 the last steam hauled train from Caerleon waits at the down platform. The shape of things to come as Diesel Class D800 loco hauls an express through Caerleon.

April 30th 1962, departing to Newport for the last time by scheduled steam. Hauled by *'Prairie'* class locomotive, passing under Lodge Road Bridge.

Plymouth-Manchester express passing 'Star Brickworks' Summer 1958, just about to pass under the Caerleon-Ponthir Road Bridge. British Railways 'Britannia Class', locomotive heads a mixed collection of coaches and a 'Dodge' lorry is seen in the right. The vehicle had not quite the company address as Ponthir when the registered address was Caerleon?

1939 another type of GWR steam locomotive. Standing first left is Fred Wagget whose family home was *'Ty Mote'*, Isca Road. Fred joined up in 1914 at 18 years of age and served for three years on the Western Front with the 1st Mons. Regiment until being discharged after suffering severe gas poisoning. He was then employed by the GWR with his fellow workers to install and maintain roadways and forecourts of the company stations throughout the western area. The roadroller was owned by the GWR and painted chocolate brown. Built by Aveling & Porter, Rochester, Kent and registered for road use on 13th November 1921, it is a 12 ton, single cylinder with slide valve. The cradle on the front is for supporting a hinged chimney so that it could be transported by rail wagon, of which there were only two specially built. The machine was registered to the Engineers Dept., Devon Place, Newport.

Diesel multiple unit stopped on down line near goods shed, 1960s.

Relics of Businesses Long Gone

Cast iron drain cover made in Caerleon by *'Richards & Hopkins'*, engineers, Iron Founders and Tin Plate manufacturers. Installed in the main surface water drainage system of *'St. Woolos Hospital'* when built as a workhouse in 1837 and still in use with others in the roadways of the hospital. The foundry was located roughly in the area now occupied by Myrtle Cottages.

Another local product, made in their millions but hidden from view in walls and buildings, their origin only to be seen when demolition occurs.

Star Brick and Tile Co. Caerleon 1950s. Two prominent skyline chimneys each being 190 feet high; the *'Star Bricks'* chimney was demolished many years ago. In the foreground are straw baled bricks.

Lightning strike on a chimney at Star Trading Estate in February 1995 because thieves had stolen approximately 20 feet of copper lightning conductor. A hole was blown in the chimney and a considerable quantity of brickworks damaged together with damage to cars and nearby buildings.

'Argosy Coachworks', Ponthir Road, 1965. Constructed in 1964-65, it is now the site of *'Star'* motorist centre, *'Just Beds'* and *'Spar Supermarket'* and filling station.

Hanbury Brewery 1/2 pint Green Glass Bottle in perfect condition after 100 years. The bottle was found in a hedgerow at Llanhenock it being made by the South Wales Glass Company Ltd., Crindau, Newport, Mon.

Ponthir Road Service Station Development Through The Years

Left: Aerial view of Ponthir Road premises late 1950s with factory sheds and disused chimney of *'Brades'* in the background.

Right: John Harris, senior and on his left, son Jack. They acquired the land in 1958 (now Ponthir Service Station), originally to service the fleet of haulage business lorries. Some years later the business developed into Car Service, Petrol and Car Sales closing the haulage site.

The house in the background was the Managers' House of the original 18th century tinworks which in turn became the *'Brades'*. It was demolished in 1979, when the land was purchased to expand the site and provide parking and car sales display area. June 2000 saw another change in usage when sold as a centre for conservatory sales.

Newly converted to Car and Petrol Sales, the first office was the caravan in the background in the 1950s.

No tarmac on the forecourt yet. Vic checks the radiator water level and brother Jack pumps fuel into the lorry loaded with 'Star' Bricks with straw between each layer - handloaded, no pallets in those days. Notice the white-wall tyres used on the recent carnival 'Ford Thames Trader' with Monmouthshire County Reg AX.

1960s and business is prospering, show rooms and offices built with the forecourt tarmaced and a Mk 10 Jaguar has just put more pounds in Jack's pocket! The business held a *'Rootes Motor Group'* franchise for marketing Hillman and Commer Vehicles.

1986 and film star Anthony Hopkins presents happy owner Mr. Terence O'Donoghue with the keys to his new car, Jack is pleased too. It is the first franchise sale of a new Hyundai by the company.

1988 and fellow colleagues toast the retirement of Colin Jenkins after 35 years of service.

Change of franchise to Hyundai in 1986. The next generation has grown up into the family business. Left to right: Son Brian, son Michael, Mrs. Doreen Harris (wife of Jack), Jack Harris and brother Vic Harris.

Caerleon Tin Plate Works 1756-1940

Caerleon Tin Plate Works circa 1880 (Established 1756). The pile of materials on the left are iron plates which would be coated with tin each side and hammered into thin sheets. The iron was cleansed of grease and impurities by soaking in fermented barley before the tin was attached to it. A water wheel trip hammer fed by the Afon Llwyd was used to thin the sheets before rolling mills were introduced. In 1946 it became 'The Brades' owned by William Hunt & Son, producers of agricultural and garden implements and tools. This closed in 1968.

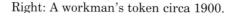

Right: A workman's token circa 1900.

Caerleon Tin Plate Works circa 1880. Many ladies were employed in the trimming and finishing process.

Reflect on the clothes and working conditions 1930.
Below: Mr. William Percival Roberts, driver, leans against the works engine, made by Manning Wardle (0-4-0) used for internal shunting of trucks loaded with tin plate to the despatch siding next to the main GWR Line, usually six at a time.

The site was first developed for large scale production using the water of the River Afon Llwyd, to work a trip hammer to beat out the plate in 1756. It continued with many changes of ownership and some periods of shutdown until its final closure in 1940. The site was then acquired in 1946 by William Hunt & Sons 'The Brades Ltd.', makers of garden implements. In 1968 they in turn, closed down and manufacturing on the site finally came to an end after more than 200 years. Housing development has since taken place, with the area named 'The Brades'. A photograph showing the early owner's home and later manager's house, can be seen in the section of Ponthir Road development.

Working Conditions of the 1920s and 1930s around the Tinplate Works

The 'Annealing' team, whereby the product is toughened by heating and slow cooling.

Health and Safety!

Cheerful in their work but what poor working
conditions.

1946, William Hunt & Sons opened their new factory. *'Brades'* factory staff 1954.
'Makers of Garden Shears for every job in the garden'.

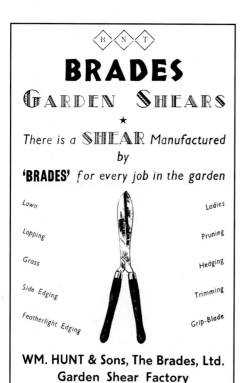

There was a lively social life centred on the canteen, with regular dances (Who were the Red Serenaders?), concerts, also bingo was played every Saturday night, with Doug Jones playing all the latest hits on the piano before and after each session. The bar was well supplied and patronised with three different breweries calling with their products.

Ann Maloney (nee Teague) who worked there until she was 17 years old remembers having her first alcoholic drink (strong shandy) there at the age of 15.

1957, left to right: Ann Philips, Betty Cavaner, Maureen Carver, Ann Maloney (nee Teague), Shirley Lewis and Winnie Lloyd. The ladies' work consisted of machine finishing, painting, packing and inspecting finished products which were shears, hammers and garden implements for onward distribution.

1957 Brades girls sitting on the wall of what is now the site of Ponthir Service Station and Car Sales. Left to right: Eileen Chantler, Maureen Carver, Shirley Lewis and Winnie Lloyd.

Local Organisations

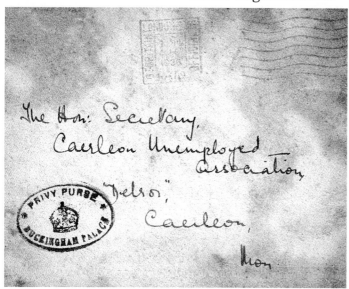

An acknowledgement from Buckingham Palace to a letter of sympathy which was sent from Caerleon Unemployed Association upon hearing the news of the death of King George V in January 1936

The 1920 and 30s were desperate days for unemployment, much of the work that was available was on an insecure basis, with lay offs and dismissal with little or no notice given. There was always a hungry man ready to fill the position if you had the nerve to protest about pay or conditions. The club members met in an upstairs room of the *'Oddfellows'* Inn, Mill Street (now demolished) where they entertained themselves with discussions, table tennis and darts etc.

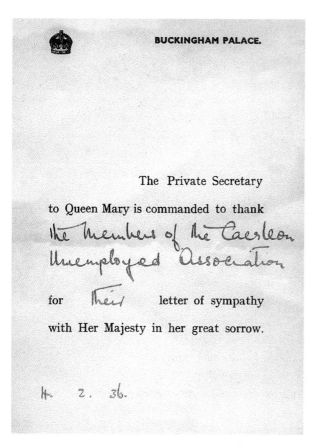

BUCKINGHAM PALACE.

The Private Secretary

to Queen Mary is commanded to thank

the members of the Caerleon Unemployed Association

for *their* letter of sympathy

with Her Majesty in her great sorrow.

4. 2. 36.

Charles Percival Richards, Honorary Secretary Caerleon Unemployed Association.

Caerleon Cricket Club 1910. Back row, left to right: F. Young, J. Taylor, H. Wallace, R. Hartland, Alf Bolton. Second row: J. Underwood, F. Rickard, C. Babbage, F. Paddimore, A. Bolton, H. Pearce, J.B. Williams and W. Hopkins. Front row: C. Bennett and R. Briton.

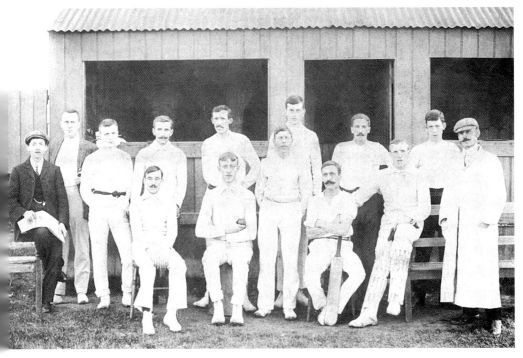

Caerleon Cricket Club Team 1906.

Soccer

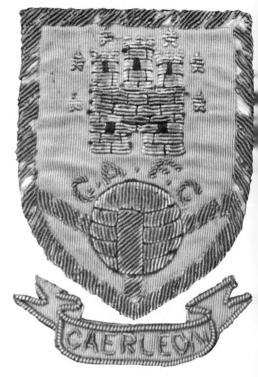

CAERLEON

ASSOCIATION FOOTBALL CLUB

FIXTURES 1937 - 1938
and
SUBSCRIPTION CARD

President ... JOHN PATON, Esq., J.P.

Chairman	... ...	J. JAMIE
Secretary	...	C. D. RICHARDS
Treasurer	...	R. K. WILLAVISE
Trainer	...	C. MERCHANT

.Committee :

C. WATTS, W. HILL, M. JENKINS

PRICE, TYP., CWMBRAN.

Caerleon Association Football Club Blazer Jacket Badge 1930s and Fixture Card 1937-38.

1937	Opponents	F	A	1938	Opponents	F	A
Sept.4..........				Jan. 1.........			
11......Pontymister			A	8......Pontymister			H
18....Pontllanfraith			A	15......Pontllanfraith			H
25.....Star Athletic			H	22......Star Athletic			A
				29......Dewstonians			A
Oct. 2.....Dewstonians			H				
9.....Trethomas			A	Feb. 5......Trethomas			H
16......1st Round Senior Bowl				12.........			
23.....				19......Crindau			A
30.....Crindau			H	26......Lliswerry			H
Nov. 6.....Lliswerry			A	Mar. 5......R.H.A. "I" Battery			A
13......R.H.A. "I" Battery			H	12......M.R.C.S. O.B.A.			H
20.....2nd Round Senior Bowl				19......Pontnewynydd Royal Blues			A
27......M.R.C.S. O.B.A.			A	26......Central Y.M.C.A.			A
Dec. 4......				April 2......Chepstow Town			A
11......Central Y.M.C.A.			H	9......Ebbw Junction			H
18......Chepstow Town			H	16.........			
25......Ebbw Junction			A	23.........			

SUBSCRIPTIONS

Name ....

Address ....

....

Ultra Pontem, *'Ashwell'* Football Team Circa 1920.

During the 1920s and 1930s there were at least three thriving football teams in Caerleon. 'Ashwell' who had a field near the tump at Ultra Pontem, *'Wesleyan Chapel'* Church Street team played on a semi regular basis, *'Caerleon A.F.C.'* who had regular fixtures and played in the Newport & District Junior League. Arthur Knorz, a player who also worked as a baker in the town, recalls that each Friday evening he would take a horse and cart out to Mr. Gibbens sawmills at Twin Oaks on the Usk Road to collect a load of sawdust, used to mark out the pitch for Saturday's game. The club strip was dark blue with gold chevron. Also a youth side called *'The Caerleon Dynamos'*.

Caerleon A.F.C. circa 1925. Back row: Johnny Hopkins, Bill Barker, Arthur Rossiter, Reg Pearce, John Strickland, M. Daley, Albert Stewart, ? Strong, ?. Middle row: Albert Young, Reg Young and Ben Barker. Front row: Tommy Edwards, Ron Rossiter, Toby Young, *'Peggy'* Dance and John Stewart.

Caerleon A.F.C. at Lovells Football Ground, Newport in 1930. They are about to play Spring Gardens A.F.C. for the Newport & District Junior League Cup, a match which they lost 2-1.
Back row, left to right: Graham Edwards, Buster Williams, Reg Pearce, Arthur Rossiter, Ken Wilston, ? Raines, Toby Young, Alex Hall, Albert Thomas, Albert Stewart, Stan Vickery, John Hopkins, ? Dantry, ? Starkey. Middle row: Reg Young, Albert Young, M. Daley, *'Punch'* Marchant. Front row: Tom Edwards, Ron Rossiter, Arthur Knorz, Freddie Williams and John Stewart.

Caerleon A.F.C. circa 1920 on a winning run.

Caerleon A.F.C. 1949 outside the Goldcroft Inn. An outing to Wembley to see an International football match.

Caerleon A.F.C. 'Dynamo's' Youth Team circa 1930s.

Caerleon Rugby Team 1970-71, the first full season. Formed in 1969-70, the boys played only a few games that season mostly on a field at the rear of the Priory Hotel, Caerleon.

Back row, left to right: Haydn Davies, Johnny Evans, Peter Turner, Des Watkins, Vernon Giles, Dick Parfitt, Robert Derrett, Nick Corten and Syd Wharton. Seated: Andrew Cooksey, David Bevan, Reg Lambert (Secretary), John Cecil (Captain), Harry West (Chairman), John Belli (Player of the Year), Colin Tuckwell (Fixture Secretary). Front: Chris Parker and Tim West.

Harry West was the Club's first Chairman and served until the end of 1975-76, in 1981 the Club won the Welsh District Cup, in 1998-99 were finalists, losing to Cefn Fforest by one point. A fortnight later they won the Newport District Trophy for the fifth time beating Pill Harriers in a lively final played at Rodney Parade, Newport. Vernon Giles first proposed the idea that Caerleon should have its own rugby club which is now

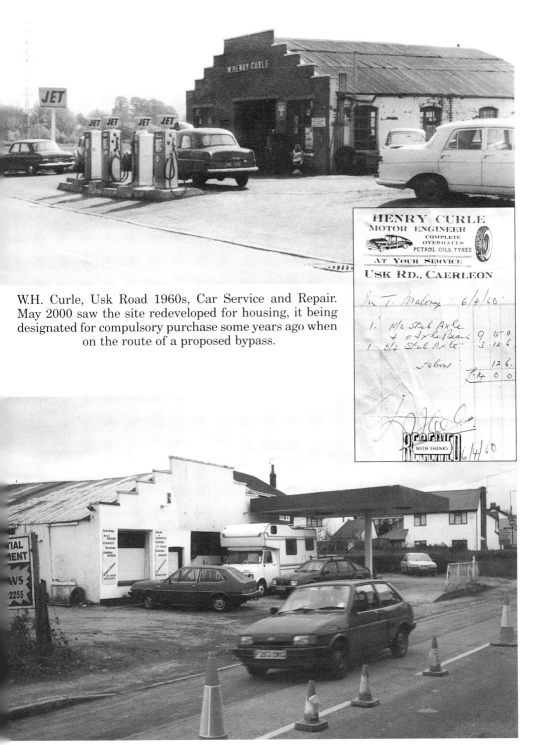

W.H. Curle, Usk Road 1960s, Car Service and Repair. May 2000 saw the site redeveloped for housing, it being designated for compulsory purchase some years ago when on the route of a proposed bypass.

July 1995 and the last days. Virtually closed with the site to be sold for housing, located opposite 'The Hawthorns'.

Gibbens Bros. until 1961 then changed to Gibbens & Sons until 1981

Gibbens Bros. (Caerleon) Ltd.

Twin Oaks Sawmills, Usk Road, Caerleon, Mon.

Est. 1888

Tel. Caerleon 375

ENGLISH TIMBER MERCHANTS AND SAWMILLERS

Makers of Hardwood Toys, Gates & Fences etc.

WE BUY - FELL - HAUL CONVERT AND DELIVER HARDWOOD TIMBER

Careful Attention given to all Enquiries

Pre-war Bedford lorry being unloaded with 'Timber in the Round' by an ex army vehicle (Chevrolet, USA) adapted to crane use. Business ceased in the 1960s and the site later developed for housing in 1990.

Allan Lusty and Ray Gibbens, his assistant, Electrical Radio and General Engineers of Station Road. They are pictured holding a tray of exhibition samples of Cabinets for Radios and Radiograms as exhibited at Radio Olympia Exhibition, London 1938.

Photograph taken in 1938 of 'Corinium House' the family home built in 1922. The sawmills moved to Twin Oaks site about 1917, the production noise at Station Road was creating complaints. The house has now changed somewhat in appearance after being extended, modernised and divided into two dwellings.

GIBBENS & SON.

William Garfield Gibbens (1886-1954), son of John Gibbens founder of the business, and Nellie his wife, the photograph being taken in 1944.

An aerial view of Twin Oaks Sawmill in the 1960s. At this time they also had an agency for "Kencast' prefabricated concrete garages. The sawmill business was sold in 1981 to John Moores, it then closed in 1990 and the site redeveloped for housing, thus ending the family's last connection after 102 years.

August 1938 at the sawmill, Ted, Bob, Ray with Minnie Gibbens steering, admiring the boat built by Ray.

Mill Street

Site of the Gwent Ambulance H.Q. before it amalgamated with other ambulance services to form a part of the Gwent Area Health Authority. Prior to this, the prefabricated building was used by the Monmouthshire County Council as offices and a Marriage Registry facility.

Signs of rundown as new houses in Cambria Close gradually encircle the workshops and garages.

'Vale View House' in the yard of the ambulance headquarters, built as an infirmary when Cambria House was built as an industrial school in 1858, by the 'Newport Board of Guardians of the Poor'. They were under the Amendment Act of 1834 extending the Caerleon Workhouse, to take in orphans and unwanted boys to train them for work! These were largely drawn from the local valleys.

During the Spanish Civil War 1936-39 it became a children's home for Basque children orphaned by the conflict. Some stayed in the area, married and their descendants still live in Caerleon. Monmouthshire County Council bought the industrial school and hospital in September 1938. During the 1939-45 war all the premises were commandeered by the Army and used as an officers' mess, wounded rehabilitation centre and storage facility with a section used for the Health Department and the emerging Monmouthshire Ambulance Service. In 1974 with the construction of County Hall the building was vacated. Cambria House was demolished in 1982 and 'Vale View' in 1999. The area was redeveloped for housing, a fine building lost that could have enjoyed much use by the community as a library and social centre.

Christmas Party 1968, for children of Monmouthshire Ambulance staff. This was held in the old village hall, which has since been demolished and now the site of retired persons bungalows and flats.

The Spanish Civil War touches Caerleon

Basque boys, refugees of the Spanish Civil War at Caerleon Town Hall preparing the defences against bombing during World War Two.

Basque boys and girls proudly display their national costumes.

BASQUE BOYS ON A.R.P.

— ◆ : ✳ : ◆ —

Experience Gained in Spanish War

A GROUP of Basque Boys who are staying at Caerleon have expressed their views on our wartime precautions in the light of their own experiences during the Spanish war.

They say that earth used for sandbags should not contain stone, as an explosion might break the bags, and then the stones might fly out and hit people. Pure sand, escaping from the bags in such a case, would do no harm. In Bilbao, when sand-bags were used to protect a building, they said, the building was reinforced from within by steel supports to enable it to resist the weight of sand. Similarly, steel supports should be placed between each layer of sand-bags. The principle is the same as that of the props used in mines to prevent the roof from falling.

ZIG-ZAG TRENCHES

The Basque boys are enthusiastic supporters of the idea of digging trenches in zig-zag formation. Such trenches, they say, are, apart from deep underground shelters, the best protection from bombs. They are cheap and easy to construct, as they need not be very deep; in fact, they say, very deep trenches may be dangerous, because in case a person is buried alive, he cannot extricate himself unless he is very near the surface of the ground.

On the other hand, a shallow trench gives adequate protection against everything except a direct hit. Even a direct hit would only kill the people in one section of the trench, provided the zig-zag formation was observed.

Above: Maria Fernandez.
On the right an article from S.W. Argus on 14th September 1939.

One of the people who sheltered the young refugees during the bitter Spanish Civil War died in January 2001 aged 97 years.

Maria Fernandez was the daughter of an ironworker from Bilbao who came to Dowlais when the British iron and steel industry began advertising for workers in Spain after the Boer War. Maria had lived only yards from Cambria House where the young refugees were housed.

Mrs. Fernandez' death severed one of the last links between South Wales and the Spanish Civil War, a conflict which saw many men from the mining villages make their way to Spain to fight for the Republican government against Franco's insurgents.

As the war grew in bitterness and intensity Franco made use of German and Italian air power to bomb the Basque towns. A steady trickle of boys were shipped from Spain to Cambria House, then under the ownership of Monmouthshire County Council. Maria's husband Manuel was a sailor and as such very often away from home. Maria with time on her hands offered her services. A lady who had looked after them before was very strict and did not like the Basque children to mix with the locals. Maria encouraged them to play together and told the Basque children that they were to be good ambassadors for their homeland and they generally took notice.

When in later years Cambria House was used as billeting space for British troops, most of the residents either found work or were adopted. Almost all of the children from the home still kept in touch with the Spanish lady they saw almost as a mother. At Christmastime her mantelpiece was covered with cards from her 'family' many of whom went on to distinguish themselves in Welsh life.

Long after she retired when asked why she did it, her reply was *'It is simple - I believed in the Spanish republic and I have always loved the people'*. What a remarkable lady.

A picture from 1936 of a Basque Boys display team with national costume and flag. Left to right: F. Antonio, Jose Mari, E. Emilio, J. Gabriel, Antonio Ansensio, Jose Luis Acha, Paeo Andres, Andres Benavente, Alberto Andres and Carlos Acha.

Basque Boys Football Team 1937-38. Left to right, Back row: Juan Bilbao, ? Gabrie, A. Manuel, G. Rufino, G. Enrique, Jules Hyles, Antonio Ansensio, S.H. Gibbon (Trainer). Front row: E. Emilio, P. Climundo, T. Luis Acha, Juan Antonio, Carlos Acha, E. Frederico.

A Christmas party held for the Basque children at Cambria House 1938-39.

Basque children and adult helpers in the yard at 'Cambria House'. Mrs. Fernandez 'Care Co-ordinator' is on the right in dark clothing with white collar markings. Jack Williams M.B.E., Chairman of Caerleon Urban District Council on the left wearing chain of office. In the early 1940s the house was closed and children dispersed to foster homes and a few were at 18 Cross Street, Caerleon for many years.

Odd Scraps of History

Remains of 'The Red Lion' Inn, Coach House and Stables. Built in 1800 it was subsequently demolished in the 1970s.

CAERLEON, MONMOUTHSHIRE.

TO BE LET,

WITH IMMEDIATE POSSESSION, IF REQUIRED,

ALL that established and well-accustomed Licensed PUBLIC-HOUSE, the Red Lion, at present in the occupation of Mr. John Jones, who leaves in consequence of a recent family bereavement.

The above House is both roomy and convenient, containing two excellent parlours; kitchen, with bar; pantries; lodge-room, 69 feet, by 15, with two fire-places; spacious brew-house, fitted with large copper furnace, iron boiler, force-pump, &c.; working-cellar, communicating by a trap-door with a roomy store-cellar; and over the brew-house a good malt-room. Behind the house is a large yard, in which are two good stables, extensive shed and pigsties, and has an entrance from the street, secured by large folding doors.

An extensive walled garden, well stocked, may be had with the premises, if required; also, 50 acres of the best meadow land, in the neighbourhood, on reasonable terms.

Rent of House, with Garden, £30., per annum; or without ditto, £25. per annum.

The incoming will not exceed from £230. to £240. There is an Oddfellows' Lodge, of 80 members, held at the house, and an Annual Woman's Club Feast of 90 members.

The line of the contemplated railway to Monmouth will be commenced early in the ensuing Spring, when this house will be most advantageously situated for any Railway Contractor.

For particulars, apply, (if by letter prepaid,) to Mr. H. M. Partridge, Auctioneer, House and Estate Agent, St. Woollos House, Stow Hill, Newport.

NEWPORT, MONMOUTHSHIRE.

TO BE SOLD BY AUCTION,

By Mr. H. M. Partridge,

At the Westgate Inn, Newport, on Wednesday, the 27th day of January, 1847, at Three o'clock in the afternoon, subject to conditions to be then produced, and in the following lots.

Lot 1.— A LL that valuable Freehold Property, situate on

---

in the box in Church from January to April 26th:—Nos. 2, 1/-; 16, 3/-; 20, 4/-; 24, 3/- 28, 7/-; 38, 3/-; 41, 1/-; 44, 1/-; 53, 7/-; 54, 1/- 55, 2/-; 60, 2/-; 65, 6/-; 81, 3/-; 87, 1 -; 88, 4/- 96, 1/6; 98, 4/-; 105, 3/-; 110, 2/-; 113, 2/- 116, 3/-; 130, 2/-; 166, 2/-; also cash in box 13/8, making £4 2s. 2d.; amount previously acknowledged, £8 7s. 2d.; Total, £12 9s. 4d

Supplies of numbered envelopes can be obtained by any applicant placing a card, with name and address, in the box.

Baptisms.

Apr.	24	Phyllis Marion Burnell Higgs.
"	24	Francis Reginald Burnell Higgs.
"	24	Eileen Mabel Burnell Higgs.
"	24	Alicia Jessie Burnell Higgs.
"	24	William Swinfield Burnell Higgs.
"	24	Leonard Douglas Burnell Higgs.
"	30	Percival George Danter.

Marriage.

Apr. 13 Eli George Young & Violet White.

Burial.

Apr. 8 Ann Young, aged 86 years.

ng & Stationery, W. Iles, 8 Caerleon Road.

Caerleon Parish Magazine.

PRICE TWO PENCE.] [MAY, 1925.

CHURCH SERVICES.

The Holy Communion—every Sunday at 8 a.m. On Great Festivals, also at 7 a.m. for 6.45 a.m. as announced. On Holy Days at 8 a.m. (or 10 a.m. as announced). Wednesdays and Fridays, 8 a.m.

Matins and Sermon—every Sunday at 11. Evensong and Sermon—every Sunday at 6.

Children's Service (Litany and Sermon) 3rd Sunday at 2.30 p.m. Matins daily at 8. Evensong daily at 6.30 (Thursdays at 5.30). Holy Baptism on Fridays at 6.30 p.m. On 3rd Sunday at 2.30 p.m.

Notice of Baptisms, Churchings, Banns, Marriages and Burials, to be given to the Vicar.

The Church is open daily for Private Prayer and Meditation.

St. Cadoc's Parish Magazine for May 1925. With the baptisms was discount given for large quantities?

Families and Personalities

December 1928 and the Miles family get together. Back, left to right: Jack, Charlie and George. Front: Mrs. Miles (Senior), Mrs. Elizabeth Miles and Mr. Bill Miles (Senior) posing under the 'Roman Arch' a garden feature built for Mrs. Elizabeth Morgan of the 'Priory' around 1820.

Jack Miles lived at 12 Church Street and worked as a bricklayer and jobbing builder in the Caerleon area. He didn't own a van and it was a common sight to see him pushing his bicycle loaded with ladders and buckets of cement hanging from the handlebars going to his next job. Ken his son, has a strong agricultural interest and for many years kept a small holding of 3 acres behind Cambria House and 3 acres at Usk which was used for raising hay. The land behind Cambria House was used for keeping 6 bullocks for fattening and 2 going for slaughter in rotation of replacement. Also chickens and 14 goats kept for milk. This was to supply a number of customers where cows milk was unsuitable for those who suffered from asthma.

Cold Bath Road, September 1999. Ken (Ike) Miles and his beloved tractor, a familiar sight together with his spaniel dogs around Caerleon over many years.

For years Ken has used his tractor in all weathers sometimes wrapped in a sack for protection from the rain. Although he gave up his small holding when the land was developed for housing he can still be seen pottering around the area doing small jobs or collecting flotsam timber from the riverbank. This keeps his house heated free throughout the winter using his wood burning stove. After many years living in Mill Street he has now come back to live in the family home in Church Street.

Wilfred Wilson, water colour artist at work on a commission in the Square at Caerleon in September 1998. Born in Newport in 1918, he came to live in Caerleon after the 1939-45 war, in which he served as a trooper in the Royal Wiltshire Yeomanry; he started by riding horses and was retrained as a tank driver driving Sherman and Crusader tanks, seeing service in the Middle East at El-Alamein and Monte Casino, Italy. He subsequently worked at and was a Director of 'Cordy's Newport, Gentlemans Outfitters', retiring in 1989. Wilfred took up painting at the end of the war and studied at the Newport College of Art. He has painted many local scenes and has a large appreciative following. His line of wash prints grace many homes worldwide.

Trooper Wilson (glasses) and crew of Sherman Tank 'Melksham' (named after the town in Wiltshire).

10th December 1996 and Gareth Jenkins decorates the shop with Christmas lights with Carole Stevens telling him to smile for the camera!

May 1999, Gareth Jenkins and Mavis Kelly of the ironmongers, High Street. 'What we don't stock we will get for you'. Real old fashioned service with friendly courtesy and advice in a well stocked emporium. Another asset to the town, 'Use it or Lose it!' is a truism for us all.

Rates: Where the monies came and went!

WEDNESDAY, JULY 17, 1912.

STATEMENT OF ACCOUNTS.

CAERLEON URBAN DISTRICT COUNCIL.

ABSTRACT OF ACCOUNTS FOR THE YEAR ENDED THE 31st DAY OF MARCH, 1912.

RECEIPTS.	£	s.	d.	EXPENDITURE.			£	s.	d.
From General District Rate at 1s. 8d. in the £	552	15	0	Maintenance, Improvement, and Enlargement of Main Roads			175	15	10
From the County Council—				Repair and Improvement of other Roads and Streets other than main roads			92	14	1
In respect of salaries of Medical Officer of Health and Inspector of Nuisances	23	15	0	Scavenging			24	0	0
In respect of Main Roads under Section II. (2) of the Local Government Act, 1888	160	0	0	Sewerage			9	13	0
Other Receipts—				Watering of Roads			9	0	2
Common Rents	1	0	0	Public Lighting			127	6	1
Miscellaneous			5	Election Expenses			9	11	0
				Legal Expenses			1	11	0
				Waterworks			7	5	1
				Salaries—					
				Medical Officer of Health and Inspector of Nuisances	80	0	0		
				Other Officers and Assistants	57	0	0		
							137	0	0
				Establishment Charges			33	14	2
				Miscellaneous Expenditure			18	0	10
				Other Contributions—					
				Newport Corporation Water Supply, Repairs to Hydrants, etc.			15	15	8
				Other Payments—					
				Notification of Infectious Diseases	1	5	0		
				Disinfectants	3	1	1		
				Lists of Births and Deaths	14	6			
							5	0	7
				Balance brought forward from previous Financial Statement			22	16	10½
				Balance in Treasurer's hands	41	0	11		
				„ „ Surveyor's hands	2	3	11½		
				„ „ Collector's hands	5	1	2		
							48	6	0½
	737	10	5				737	10	5

Rateable Value of the District according to the Poor Rate Valuation List in force at the commencement of the year, £9,239; Assessable Value of the District according to the General District Rate made next before the commencement of the year, £7,133.

(Signed) T. R. P. HERBERT, Clerk to the Urban District Council.
5th July, 1912.

I hereby certify that I have compared the entries in the above Statement with the Vouchers and other documents relating thereto, and that the Regulations with respect to such Statement have been duly complied with.

I hereby further certify that I have ascertained by Audit the correctness of such Statement, and that the expenditure of the District Council during the year ended the 31st day of March, 1912, included in such Statement and allowed by me at the Audit is £666 7s. 6d.

As witness my hand this 13th day of July, 1912.

(Signed) M. D. PROPERT, District Auditor.

May 1999 Gino Alonzi outside his salon in Station Road. He opened for business in 1969 and is still going strong.

Ready for a jungle patrol serving in Malaya with the South Wales Borderers from 1955 to 1957.

A steady hand with the razor. A trendy short back and sides with nothing off the top!

1920 Arthur Green born in a house which is now part of the 'Goldcroft Inn' in 1868, passing away in 1935. He joined the Alexandra (Newport and South Wales) Docks and Railway Co. as Constable and later promoted to Sergeant. Left to right, rear: Margaret Rose Green (Daughter), Trevor Green (son) and Nell Green (Daughter). Front: Arthur Green (Father), Hilda Green (Daughter) and Margaret Green (Mother). His father was a tin plate manufacturer in Caerleon and grandfather was the Caerleon Postmaster with his premises in Cross Street.

Arthur Green in the dress uniform of First Officer, in the Alexandra Docks Division of the St. John Ambulance Brigade circa 1912. Wearing the Service Medal, awarded for conspicuous service to the Order of St. John of Jerusalem in England. The Alexandra Docks Division existed only until 1917.

Mr. William Powell 1895-1971.

In 1929 he was awarded *'The Carnegie Hero Fund Trust Certificate for Heroism'*, for the part he played in efforts to rescue a workmate trapped in a main sewer in Maindee, Newport, Mon.

He crawled through the sewer from Christchurch Road to Fair Oak Avenue, to get to the trapped man. He was also presented with an inscribed silver pocket watch by the Mayor of Newport, on behalf of the Municipal Insurance Co. *'In Appreciation of His Gallant Efforts to Save the Life of his Workmate Thomas Williams.'*

During the First World War he served with the Royal Field Artillery in Egypt. During the Second World War he was a Staff Officer in the Air Raid Precautions Organisation (A.R.P.). He worked for 36 years for Newport County Borough, many years as a Foreman and served his Caerleon Community as Councillor with the Caerleon Urban District Council for three years. In the 1920s he lived at Penrhos Cottage, and in 1951 he became inn keeper at the Drovers Arms where he lived until his death in 1971. The photograph above shows him carrying the mace, in a mock parliament held at the Civic Centre, Newport.

Able Seaman Charles Leonard Watkins, Royal Navy, born 23rd November 1923 at Hawthorn Cottage, Usk Road, Caerleon. The youngest of five sons born to Elizabeth and Frederick Watkins, living in Caerleon all his life and attending Caerleon Endowed School, he was very artistic and loved to draw, winning many competitions for painting and penmanship. A furniture company of Newport, 'Barlows' donated prizes for outstanding work and Charlie received one of the prizes.

He was a keen churchgoer and along with his brothers Aubrey, Arthur and Cyril was a choirboy at St. Cadoc's Church. Charlie took up an apprenticeship with Mr. Gibbens at Twin Oak, timber yard on the Usk Road as a carpenter until he was called up at 19 years of age.

In 1942 he joined the Royal Navy at Devonport, Plymouth and his first duties after training were two voyages to Murmansk in arctic Russia, on convoy escort duties. His ship was then sent to the Mediterranean to silence coastal gun batteries in preparation for the Anzio landing in Italy. His ship the flotilla leader, H.M.S. Inglefield was sunk off Nettuno, a short distance from the Anzio beachhead at dusk on the 25th February 1944 by a Heinkel 111, launched radio controlled glider bomb. Out of the ships company of 178, 157 were saved.

Early in March 1944 his parents received their first notification that their son, Able Seaman D/JX 365 319 Charles Leonard Watkins was missing, on the 28th March they received confirmation that he had lost his life serving his country.

Later letters of condolence were received from H.M. King George VI and The Commodore, H.M.S. Drake, Plymouth. A memorial certificate and letter of sympathy and gratitude for his sacrifice were presented by Caerleon Urban District Council on behalf of the people of Caerleon. His name together with other men from Caerleon who lost their lives in both wars can be found engraved on the Cenotaph sited in the Memorial Gardens and also at St. Cadoc's Church over the main door.

The above photograph was taken at Devonport on completion of his training.

The Destroyer, H.M.S. Inglefield.

Royal Naval Barracks,
DEVONPORT.

28th March, 1944.

Dear Sir,

        With reference to my letter of the 13th March,
1944, it is with deep regret that I have to inform you
that it has now become necessary to presume that your Son,
Charles Leonard Watkins, Able Seaman, D/JX.365319, lost
his life on the 25th February 1944, whilst on war service,
consequent on the loss of H.M.S.'INGLEFIELD'.

        Please allow me to express on behalf of the
Officers and Men of the Royal Navy, the high traditions
of which your Son has helped to maintain, sincere sympathy
with you in your sad loss.

        Yours sincerely,

COMMODORE.

Mr. F.Watkins,
Glenview,
Carlton Tce;
Caeleon, Mon.

BUCKINGHAM PALACE

      The Queen and I offer you our
heartfelt sympathy in your great
sorrow.

      We pray that your country's
gratitude for a life so nobly given
in its service may bring you some
measure of consolation.

George R.I.

F. Watkins Esq.

To the Family of

C. Watkins

who gave his Life serving in Britain's Fighting Forces
during the

World War
September 1939, to August 1945.

~

We, the People of Caerleon

extend Heartfelt Sympathy, and Honour with Pride the
Valour of our Sons and Daughters, whose Steadfast=
ness, Courage and Sacrifice prevailed against Evil and
shielded us from Subjugation.

"And with the Passing of the Ones we Love
So dies a little part of us."

The year is 1959 and top left can be seen the Riding School Field with the Stables. Beyond are bare fields before the opening of 'East Lyne Garden Centre' on the Usk Road.

Again 1959 and upper left the prefabs are still in place. Clearly seen on right middle ground is the site of the future Castle

May 1959 and the Roman Ampitheatre shows up well, the serpentine nature of the River Usk's course is easily seen.

May 1958: a chalk fan across all views of Cowdeen

Acknowledgements

t is with sincere thanks that I readily give credit to those who generously allowed the loan of photographs and gave of their own time and knowledge.

Photographs: - Gino Alonzi, Lily Avery, Mrs. Josephine Allaman (nee Davies) British Columbia, Stephen Berry (Newport), Val Burnell-Jones (nee Higgs), Marjorie Bennett, Leon Bond (Newport), D. Burnicle (Photographer), Jim Blythe (Ultra Pontem), Bryn Collier (Ponthir), Alan Cox (Cardiff), Monica and Brian Donahue (Newport), Ian Evans Information Librarian Newport C.B.), Alice Eddols (nee Shierson), Maureen and Anthony Friend (Newport), Julie Ann Ford, Elsie Gibbens, Royce Gardener (Sheriff of Caerleon, Retired), Marion Gardener, Carol Graves (Reference Library Newport C.B.), M.E. Green, Allan Grant (Artist and Author, Newport), Derek Gear (Tredunnock), Vic Harris, Doreen Harris, Brian Harris, Dorothy Haynes (Newport), David Hall (Ponthir), Audrey Hemming, Tony Herbert (Newport), Dorothy Jeffrey, Margaret Jones, Mary Jackson (nee Williams), Rev. R.W.A. Jones, M.Sc. F.R.S.C. (Newport Pembs.), David and Carol Jones (Caerleon Post Office), Arthur Knorz, James Kirkwood (Councillor) F.R.S.A., Ann and Terry Maloney, Lynette Morris (nee Avery), Gordon Murray, Ken Miles, Ashuk Miah, Jeff Mears (Asst. Div. Officer S.W. Fire Brigade), Barbara Needham (nee Gulley), National Museum of Wales, Ron Pearce, Susan Pugh (Reference Library Newport C.B.), Mrs. Amy Prosser, Mrs. R.A. Richards, Lyn Richards, Barry Richards (Graphic Designer, Caerleon), the late Godfrey Rowlands, Ken Rees, Janet Ripley, William (Bill) Roberts, Salladur Rahman, Liz Sullivan, Doug Slater (Newport), Alan Sorrell A.R.W.S., Glyn Teague, Doreen Trickey (Llanhennock), Nancy Wollan, Wilfred Wilson (Artist), Mrs. Molly Weeks, Jim and Queenie Waggett, Henry West, Roger Waggett, Glyn Webb (Newport), Billie and Peter Williams, John Wynn (Wynns Heavy Haulage Newport), Robert Webb, Patrick White (Newport).

Time, Advice, Information and Useful Assistance: - John Abraham, Rachel Anderton (Assistant Museum Officer Newport C.B.), Kath Bryant (Newport), Joe Beddow, Jeff Bishop, Helen Baker (Newport), Katie Baggs, Mike Buckingham (South Wales Argus), Graham Cross (Artist), Ron Comfort (Senior Ambulance Officer), Keith Dunn (Executive Director St. John Ambulance in Wales), Roger Davies, Allan Dowling (Caldicot), Cynthia Evans (Newport), the late Mr. Valentine Finn, Allan Whiting (Town Hall), Graham Williams, Raymond Waller, Cyril Watkins, Sheena Webb, Paul Green (Decorator), Sioned Wyn Hughes (Asst. Curator St. Fagans Museum of Welsh Life), John Hardwick, Mr. and Mrs. G.W. Hemmings, Gwyndaf Jones, Jean Kirkwood, Thurston Lovett, Jo Lillis, Neil Leyland (South Wales Fire Brigade), Ann Lane, Ron Morgan, Tracy Pritchard and Phoebe, Derek Pring (Cwmbran), Karen Phillips (Ponthir), Jim Povell, Phillip Rollings, Dr. Russell Rees M.D., Dave Rushton, Charles de Lancey Richards, John J. Sparkes (Rogerstone), Tim Stopford (Caldicot), Bob Stedman, Bob Trett (Museums Officer Newport C.B.)., Dr. David Osmand M.B., B.Ch., P.M. Jones B.A. (Deputy Head Caerleon Comprehensive), Paul Dixon (University of Wales College Caerleon), Enrique Garay, David Rimmer (Gwent County Archivist and Search-Room Staff), John Pritchard (Engineering and Construction Division, Newport Co. Boro. Council), Louis Bannon, Nigel Young (www. Caerleon Net), Fred Wheeler (Foreman Brades).

To Assembly Member Rosemary Butler for giving her most valuable time in providing the Foreword.

My sincere appreciation to Malcolm Thomas and all the staff at Old Bakehouse Publications for their friendly and helpful advice.

Once again grateful thanks to the many who have shown interest as the above list indicates, without whose help the recording of Caerleon's history would not be possible.

Bibliography

'Guide to Caerleon-on-Usk', *W.A. Morris, Lt. Col. R.A.M.C., Retired* - Published 1931.

'R.H. Johns' Newport Directories, 1899, 1908.

Great Western Railway, Ticket Examiners, 1928 Fares Book.

'Caerleon Heritage Trail', Pamphlet - *Published by Caerleon Civic Society, Caerleon Local Histor* *Society and Gwent County Council.*

'Historic Caerleon' A Walk Around, *Pamphlet published by Caerleon Civic Society, Researched b* *P. Hockey.*

'Caerleon - Isca' *Roman Legionary Museum Booklet* - Published 1987, National Museum o Wales.

'A Popular Guide to Caerleon', *by Isca and Altwood Wood Thorne, M.B. (London),* Published 192 Western Mail.

'South Wales Argus' *various dates*

'Souvenir Programme Sat 13th June 1987 to celebrate the opening of the Legionary Museum'.

'Local Government in Newport' 1835-1935, *by John Warner F.L.A.* - Published Newpor Corporation.

'Hanbury Ale House', *Information pamphlet* - 1996.

'Historic Caerleon', *Official Guide of the Urban District Council* - 1955.

'Monmouthshire County Guide, 1954' - Published Mon. C.C. by the Home Publishing Co Croydon.

'The Story of Brynglas House', *by D.L. Anne Hobbs, research by Tony Friend* - Published b Brynglas Community Educational Centre, 1989.

'Steam in South Wales Vol. 4', *Monmouthshire by Michael Hale* - Published by Oxford Publishin Co.

'History of The Red Cross in Monmouthshire, 1910-1918', *by Robin Jones, R.G.N., A.I.C.L* - Published 1988.

'The Roman Past of Heidenheim and its Twin Town' *by Helmut Weimert* - Published Heidenhei City Archives, 1991.

'Newport Transport 80 Years of Service', *E.A. Thomas* - Published by Newport Borough Counc

'Caerleon Past and Present', *Primrose Hockey, M.B.E.*

'Caerleon Endowed School' 1724-1983, *T.M. Morgan* - Published by Starling Press 1983.

'Caerleon Endowed School' The First 270 Years, *T.M. Morgan* - Published 1994, Williams Schoo Caerleon.

Below is a selection of further titles available. Please send stamp to the Publishers for a detailec list.

Pictorial Memories of Old Pontypool - **Volume 1**
 by Bryan Roden ISBN 1 874538 86
Pictorial Memories of Old Pontypool - **Volume 2**
 by Bryan Roden ISBN 1 874538 04
Caerleon 'Scenes Past'
 by Norman Stevens ISBN 1 874538 71
The Place-Names of Eastern Gwent
 by Graham Osborne and Graham Hobbs ISBN 1 874538 91
Caldicot and the Villages of the Moor - **Volume 1**
 by Malcolm D. Jones ISBN 0 874538 50
Something Must Be Done
 by Ted Rowlands, MP ISBN 0 9539376 1
The Aneurin Bevan Inheritance
 by Gareth Jones ISBN 1 874538 17
Remember Abergavenny - **Volume 1**
 by Louis Bannon ISBN 1 874538 75
Welsh Roots and Branches
 by Gareth Jones ISBN 0 9524176 0
The District of Sennybridge - **Part 1**
 by Gareth Jones ISBN 1 874538 51
The District of Sennybridge - **Part 2**
 by Gareth Jones ISBN 1 874538 87